# BOYS

**Arranged by DAN COATES**
*for easy piano*

Project Manager: CAROL CUELLAR
Art Design: CARMEN FORTUNATO and MARTHA L. RAMIREZ

DAN COATES® is a registered trademark of WARNER BROS. PUBLICATIONS

# CONTENTS

American Pie . . . . . . . . . . . . . . . . . . . . . . . . . . . .4

The Ballad of Gilligan's Isle . . . . . . . . . . . . . . . . . . . .8

Cat's in the Cradle . . . . . . . . . . . . . . . . . . . . . . . . .11

Change the World . . . . . . . . . . . . . . . . . . . . . . . . . .16

The Flag Parade
(from *Star Wars* Episode I: *The Phantom Menace*) . . . . . . . . . .20

(Meet) The Flintstones . . . . . . . . . . . . . . . . . . . . . . .24

Give Me Just One Night (Una Noche) . . . . . . . . . . . . . . . . .70

Hotel California . . . . . . . . . . . . . . . . . . . . . . . . . .26

It's My Life . . . . . . . . . . . . . . . . . . . . . . . . . . . .32

Jeopardy Theme . . . . . . . . . . . . . . . . . . . . . . . . . . .36

Jetsons Main Theme . . . . . . . . . . . . . . . . . . . . . . . . .38

Lean on Me . . . . . . . . . . . . . . . . . . . . . . . . . . . . .40

Olympic Fanfare and Theme . . . . . . . . . . . . . . . . . . . . . .44

Return to Pooh Corner . . . . . . . . . . . . . . . . . . . . . . . .48

Smooth . . . . . . . . . . . . . . . . . . . . . . . . . . . . . . .52

Song from *M*A*S*H* . . . . . . . . . . . . . . . . . . . . . . . . .56

Thank You for Loving Me . . . . . . . . . . . . . . . . . . . . . . .58

Theme from Inspector Gadget . . . . . . . . . . . . . . . . . . . . .62

The Throne Room (from *Stars Wars*) . . . . . . . . . . . . . . . . .66

Victory Celebration (from *Return of the Jedi*) . . . . . . . . . . .73

We're Off to See the Wizard . . . . . . . . . . . . . . . . . . . . .76

# Dan Coates

**A**s a student at the University of Miami, Dan Coates paid his tuition by playing the piano at south Florida nightclubs and restaurants. One evening in 1975, after Dan had worked his unique brand of magic on the ivories, a stranger from the music field walked up and told him that he should put his inspired piano arrangements down on paper so they could be published.

Dan took the stranger's advice—and the world of music has become much richer as a result. Since that chance encounter long ago, Dan has gone on to achieve international acclaim for his brilliant piano arrangements. His Big Note, Easy Piano and Professional Touch arrangements have inspired countless piano students and established themselves as classics against which all other works must be measured.

Enjoying an exclusive association with Warner Bros. Publications since 1982, Dan has demonstrated a unique gift for writing arrangements intended for students of every level, from beginner to advanced. Dan never fails to bring a fresh and original approach to his work. Pushing his own creative boundaries with each new manuscript, he writes material that is musically exciting and educationally sound.

From the very beginning of his musical life, Dan has always been eager to seek new challenges. As a five-year-old in Syracuse, New York, he used to sneak into the home of his neighbors to play their piano. Blessed with an amazing ear for music, Dan was able to imitate the melodies of songs he had heard on the radio. Finally, his neighbors convinced his parents to buy Dan his own piano. At that point, there was no stopping his musical development. Dan won a prestigious New York State competition for music composers at the age of 15. Then, after graduating from high school, he toured the world as an arranger and pianist with the group Up With People.

Later, Dan studied piano at the University of Miami with the legendary Ivan Davis, developing his natural abilities to stylize music on the keyboard. Continuing to perform professionally during and after his college years, Dan has played the piano on national television and at the 1984 Summer Olympics in Los Angeles. He has also accompanied recording artists as diverse as Dusty Springfield and Charlotte Rae.

During his long and prolific association with Warner Bros. Publications, Dan has written many awardwinning books. He conducts piano workshops worldwide, demonstrating his famous arrangements with a special spark that never fails to inspire students and teachers alike.

# AMERICAN PIE

Words and Music by
DON McLEAN
*Arranged by DAN COATES*

**Slowy and freely**

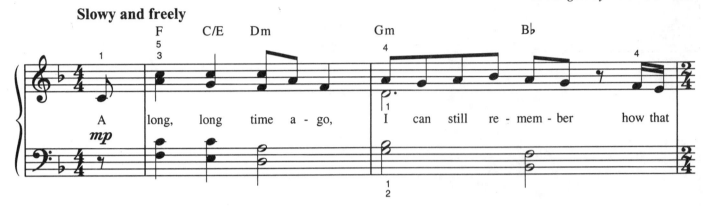

A long, long time a-go, I can still re-mem-ber how that

mu - sic used to make me smile. And I knew that if I had my chance,

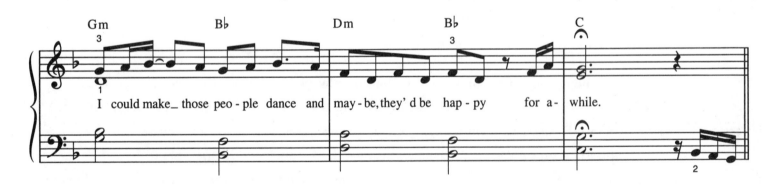

I could make_ those peo-ple dance and may-be, they'd be hap-py for a- while.

**Bright, steady beat**
*Verse:*

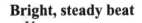

1. Did you_ write the book of love?_ And do you_ have faith in
2. *See additional lyrics*

6

both kicked off your shoes.___ Man, I dig those rhy-thm and blues. I was a

lone - ly teen - age bronc - in' buck___ with a pink car - na - tion and a

pick - up truck,___ but I knew that I was out___ of luck___ the

day the mu - sic died. I start-ed sing-in':

*cresc.*

**%** *Chorus:*

Bye - bye, Miss A - mer - i - can Pie.___ Drove my Chev - y to the lev - ee, but the

**Verse 2:**
I met a girl who sang the blues
And I asked her for some happy news,
But she just smiled and turned away.
I went down to the sacred store,
Where I heard the music years before,
But the man there said the music wouldn't play.
And in the streets, the children screamed,
The lovers cried and the poets dreamed.
But not a word was spoken;
The church bells were all broken.
And the three men I admire most,
The Father, Son, and Holy Ghost,
They caught the last train for the coast
The day the music died.
And they were singin' :
(To Chorus:)

# THE BALLAD OF GILLIGAN'S ISLE

Words and Music by
SHERWOOD SCHWARTZ and GEORGE WYLE
*Arranged by DAN COATES*

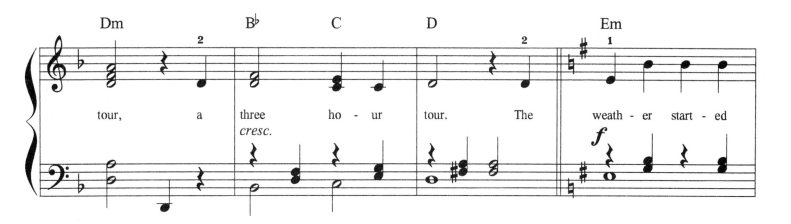

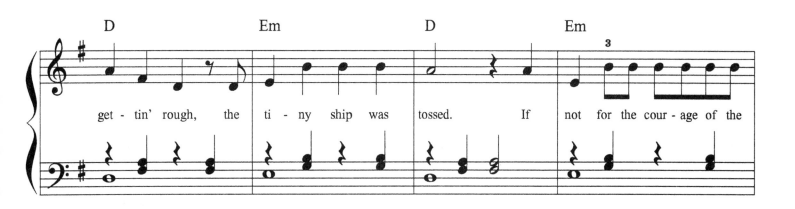

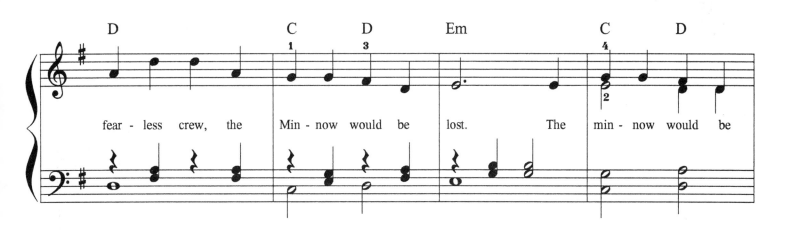

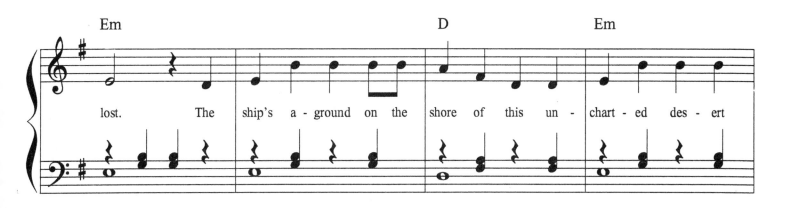

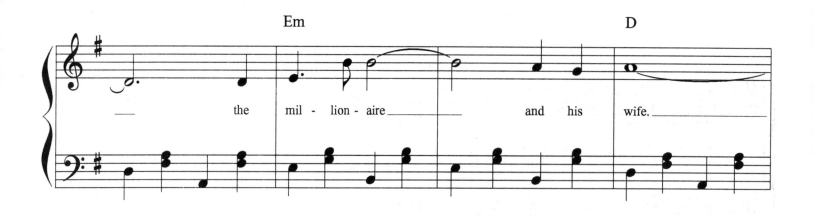

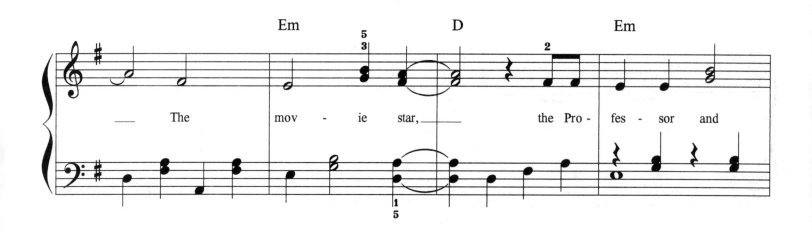

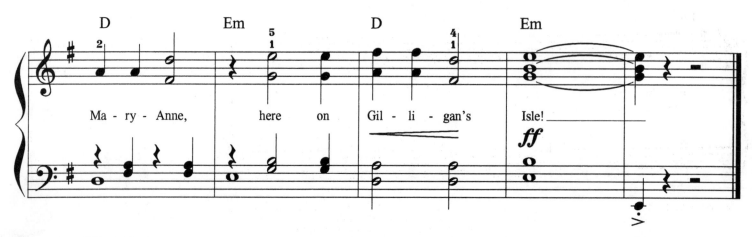

# CAT'S IN THE CRADLE

Words and Music by
HARRY CHAPIN and SANDY CHAPIN
*Arranged by DAN COATES*

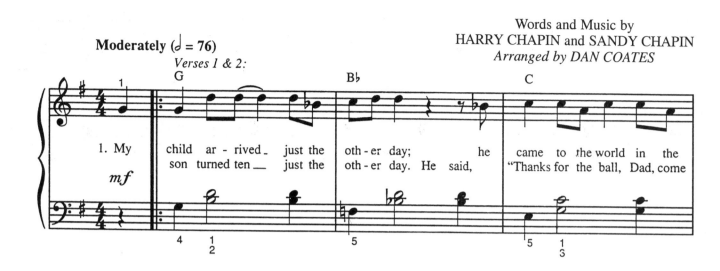

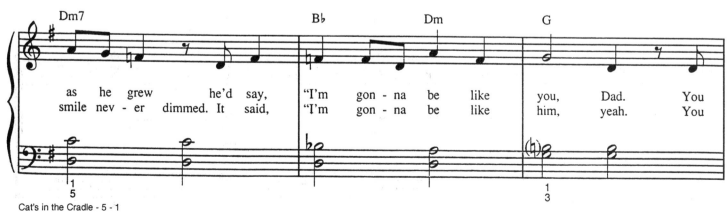

Cat's in the Cradle - 5 - 1

oth - er day, so much like a man I just had to say, ___ "Son, I'm

proud of you. ___ Can you sit for a while?" ___ He shook his head and he

said with a smile, ___ "What I'd real - ly like, Dad, is to bor - row the car ___ keys.

*D.S. 𝄋 al Coda I*

See you lat - ter. Can I have them, please?" And the

Cat's in the Cradle - 5 - 3

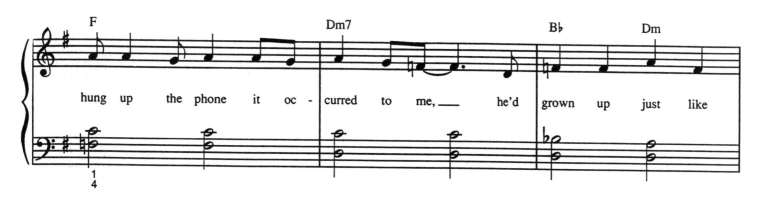

hung up the phone it oc - curred to me, \_\_\_ he'd grown up just like

me. My boy was just like me. And the

*D.S. %S al Coda II*

*Coda II*

then, Dad, we're gon - na have a good time then."

*rit.*

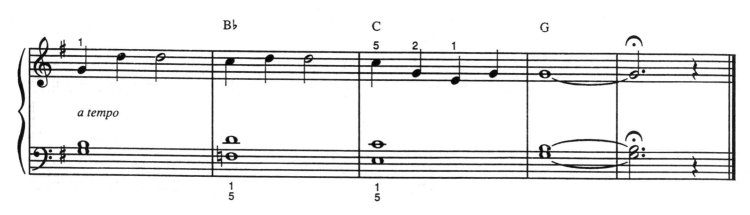

*a tempo*

# CHANGE THE WORLD

Words and Music by
TOMMY SIMS, GORDON KENNEDY
and WAYNE KIRKPATRICK
*Arranged by DAN COATES*

1. If I could reach the stars, I'd pull one down for you,
2. If I could be a king, e-ven for a day,

shine in on my heart
I'd take you as my queen.

Change the World - 4 - 1

# THE FLAG PARADE

By
JOHN WILLIAMS
*Arranged by DAN COATES*

The Flag Parade - 4 - 1

The Flag Parade - 4 - 2

# (MEET) THE FLINSTONES
## from "THE FLINTSTONES"

Words and Music by
WILLIAM HANNA, JOSEPH BARBERA
and HOYT CURTIN
*Arranged by DAN COATES*

# HOTEL CALIFORNIA

Words and Music by
DON HENLEY, GLENN FREY and DON FELDER
*Arranged by DAN COATES*

Moderate Rock beat ♩ = 128

On a dark des - ert high - way,      cool wind in my
Her mind is Tif - fa - ny twist - ed.      She got the Mer - ce - des

hair,      warm __ smell of co - li - tas
bends.      She got a lot of pret - ty, pret - ty boys

Hotel California - 6 - 1

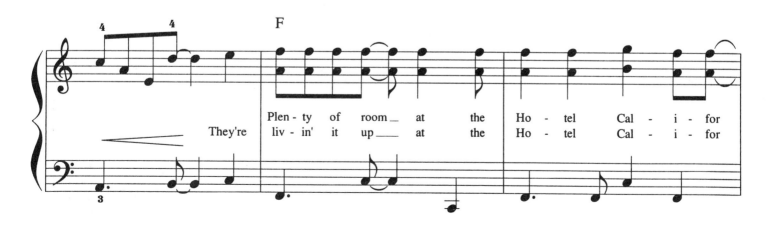

Hotel California - 6 - 4

# IT'S MY LIFE

Words and Music by
JON BON JOVI, RICHIE SAMBORA
and MAX MARTIN
*Arranged by DAN COATES*

**Steady rock beat (♩ = 120)**

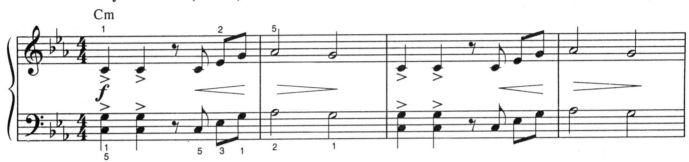

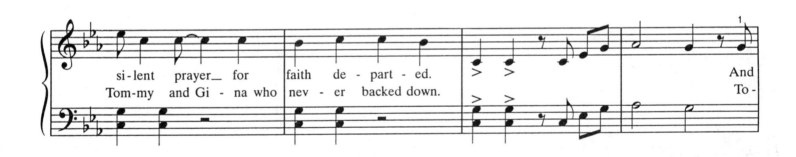

It's My Life - 4 - 1

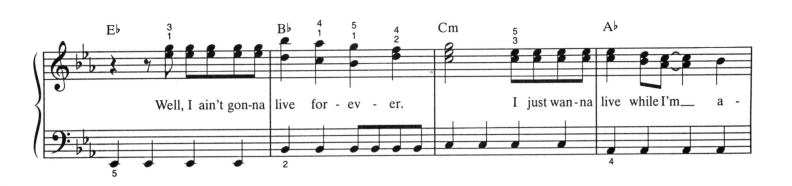

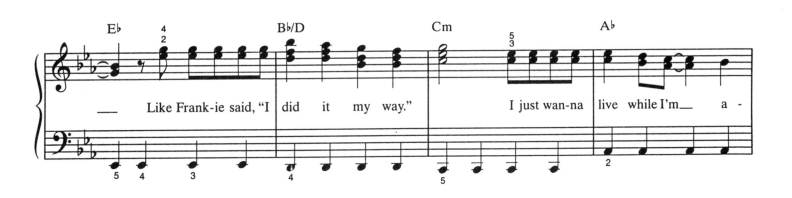

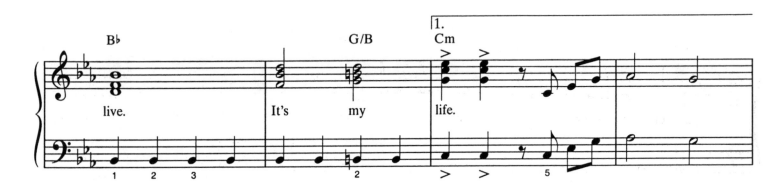

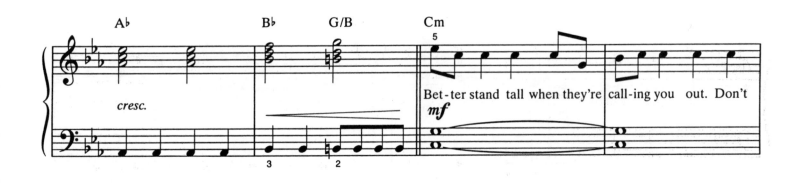

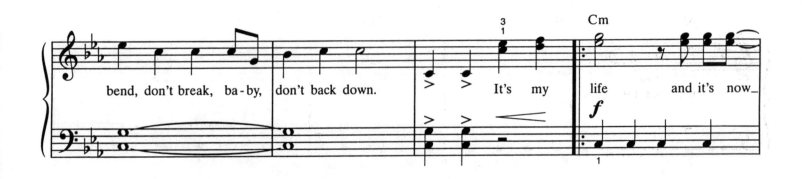

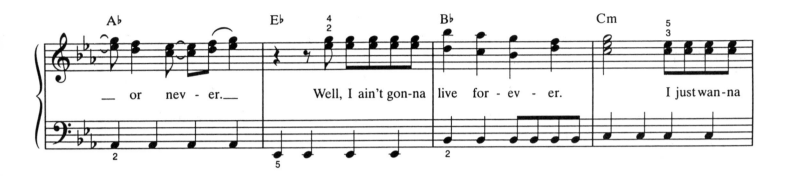

# JEOPARDY THEME

By
MERV GRIFFIN
*Arranged by DAN COATES*

**Brightly**

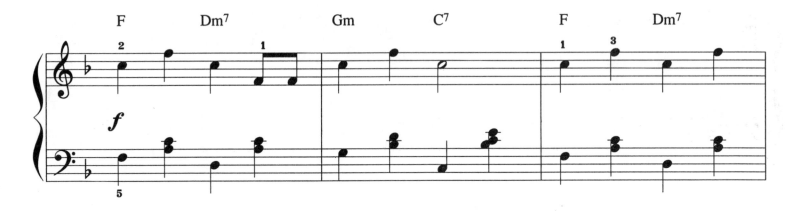

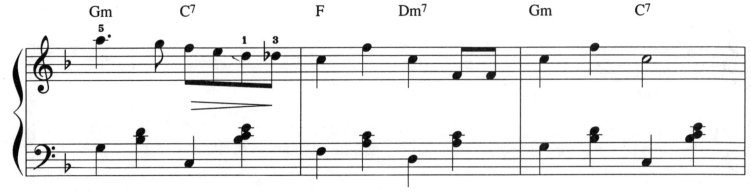

# THE JETSONS MAIN THEME
## from "THE JETSONS"

Words and Music by
WILLIAM HANNA, JOSEPH BARBERA
and HOYT S. CURTIN
*Arranged by DAN COATES*

The Jetsons Main Theme - 2 - 1

# LEAN ON ME

Words and Music by
BILL WITHERS
*Arranged by DAN COATES*

Lean on Me - 4 - 1

# OLYMPIC FANFARE AND THEME

By
JOHN WILLIAMS
*Arranged by DAN COATES*

Olympic Fanfare and Theme - 4 - 1

*Bass Note Optional

Olympic Fanfare and Theme - 4 - 2

# RETURN TO POOH CORNER

Words and Music by
KENNY LOGGINS
*Arranged by DAN COATES*

Return to Pooh Corner - 4 - 1

50

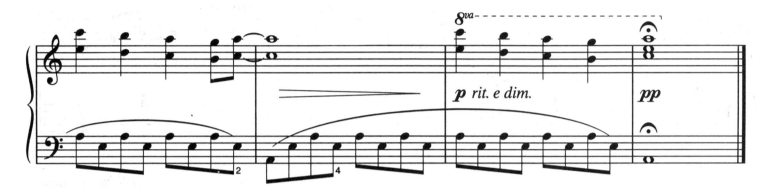

*Verse 3:*
It's hard to explain how a few precious things
Seem to follow throughout all our lives.
After all's said and done, I was watching my son
Sleeping there with my bear by his side.
So I tucked him in, I kissed him and as I was gone,
I'd swear that old bear whispered, "Boy, welcome home."
Believe me if you can, I've finally come
Back to the house of Pooh Corner by one.
And what do you know, there's so much to be done.
Count all the bees in the hive,
Chase all the clouds from the sky.
Back to the days of Christopher Robin,
Back to the ways of Christopher Robin,
Back to the days of Pooh.

# SMOOTH

Music and Lyrics by
ITAAL SHUR and ROB THOMAS
*Arranged by DAN COATES*

Smooth - 4 - 1

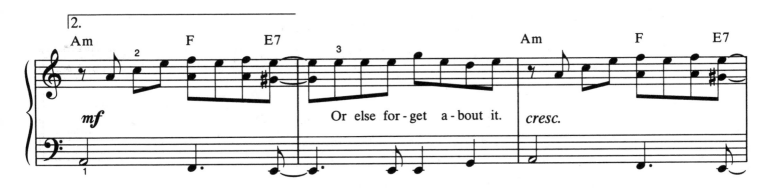

*Verse 2:*
Well, I'll tell you one thing,
If you should leave, it'd be a crying shame.
In every breath and every word
I hear your name calling me out, yeah.
Well, out from the barrio,
You hear my rhythm on your radio.
You feel the tugging of the world,
So soft and slow, turning you 'round and 'round.
And if you said this life ain't good enough,
I would give my world to lift you up.
I could change my life to better suit your mood.
'Cause you're so smooth.
*(To Chorus:)*

# SONG FROM M*A*S*H
## (Suicide Is Painless)

Words and Music by
MIKE ALTMAN and JOHNNY MANDEL
*Arranged by DAN COATES*

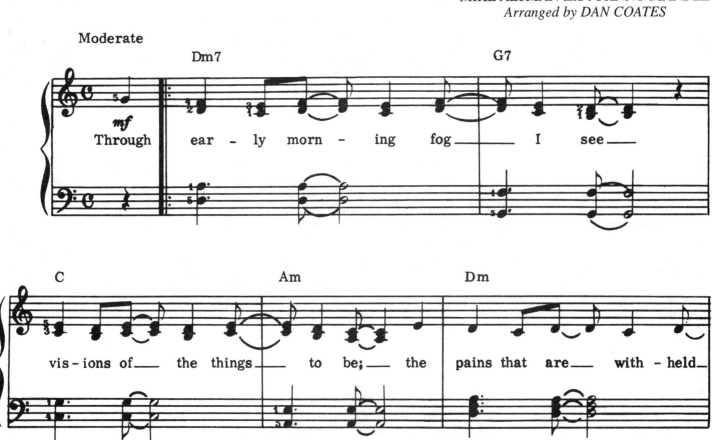

Through ear-ly morn-ing fog I see vis-ions of the things to be; the pains that are with-held

for me. I re-al-ize and I can see

that su-i-cide is pain-

Song From "M*A*S*H" - 2 - 1

1. Try to find a way to make
   All our little joys relate
   Without that ever-present hate
   But now I know that it's too late.
   And -(Chorus)

3. The game of life is hard to play,
   I'm going to lose it anyway,
   The losing card I'll someday lay,
   So this is all I have to say,
   That -(Chorus)

4. The only way to win, is cheat
   And lay it down before I'm beat,
   And to another give a seat
   For that's the only painless feat.
   'Cause: -(Chorus)

5. The sword of time will pierce our skins,
   It doesn't hurt when it begins
   But as it works its way on in,
   The pain grows stronger, watch it grin.
   For: -(Chorus)

6. A brave man once requested me
   To answer questions that are key,
   Is it to be or not to be
   And I replied; "Oh, why ask me."
   'Cause: -(Chorus)

Song From "M*A*S*H" - 2 - 2

# THANK YOU FOR LOVING ME

Words and Music by
JON BON JOVI and RICHIE SAMBORA
*Arranged by DAN COATES*

**Slowly** (♩ = 66)

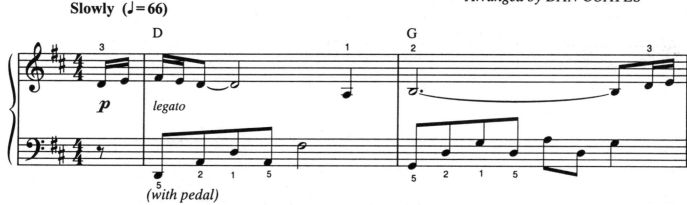

*Verse:*

hard for me to say the things I want to say some - times. There's

nev - er knew I had a dream, un - til that dream was you.

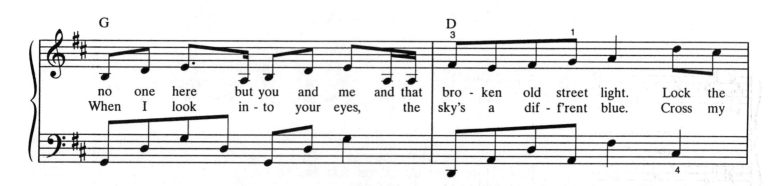

no one here but you and me and that bro - ken old street light. Lock the

When I look in - to your eyes, the sky's a dif - f'rent blue. Cross my

Thank You for Loving Me - 4 - 1

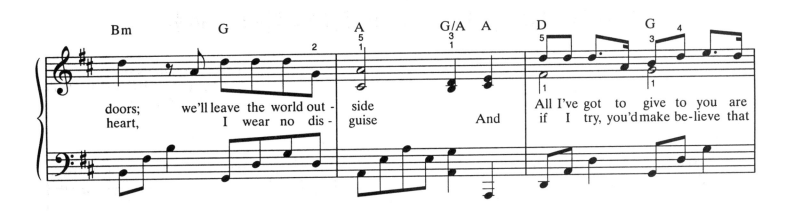

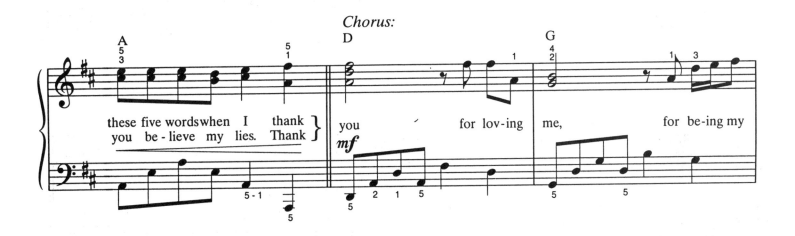

Thank You for Loving Me - 4 - 2

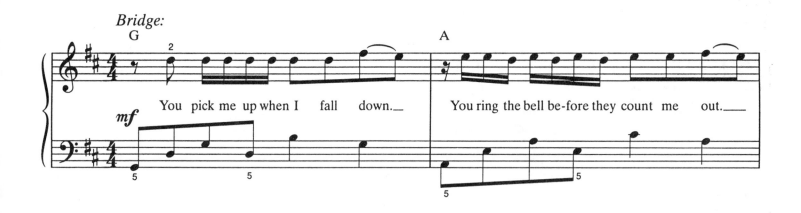

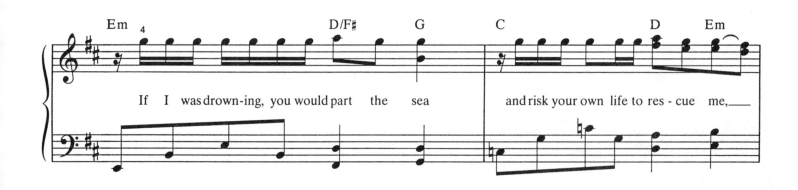

# THEME FROM INSPECTOR GADGET
## (Animated Cartoon Series)

Words and Music by
HAIM SABAN and SHUKI LEVY
*Arranged by DAN COATES*

Theme From Inspector Gadget - 4 - 1

# THE THRONE ROOM

Music by
JOHN WILLIAMS
*Arranged by DAN COATES*

**Majestically** ( ♩ = 120 )

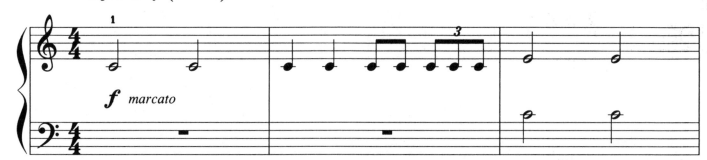

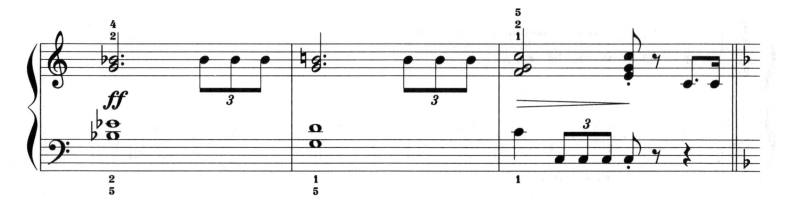

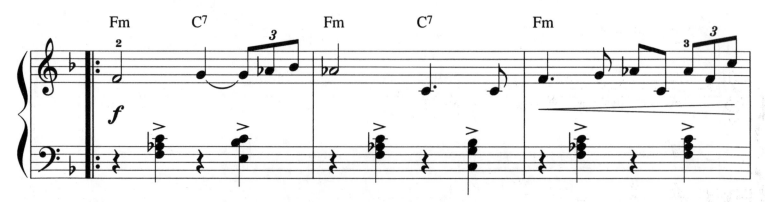

The Throne Room - 4 - 1

# GIVE ME JUST ONE NIGHT
## (UNA NOCHE)

Words and Music by
CLAUDIA OGALDE, ANDERS BAGGE
and ARNTHOR BIRGISSON
*Arranged by DAN COATES*

**Moderately fast (♩ = 124)**

*Verse 1:*

1. Your lips keep tell-ing me you want me,_____ and hold me close all through the

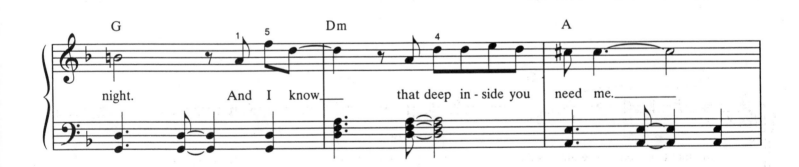

night. And I know____ that deep in-side you need me.____

*Verses 2 & 3:*

No one else can make it right.

2. Don't you try to hide your
3. Your eyes with pas-sion make me

Give Me Just One Night - 3 - 1

I'll give you the time of your life.

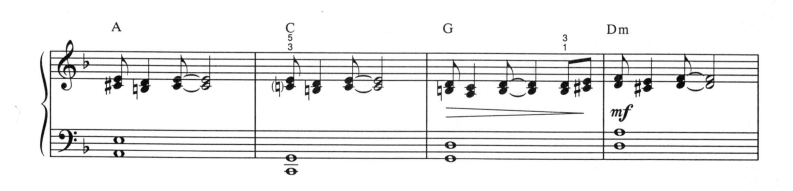

*To Coda*

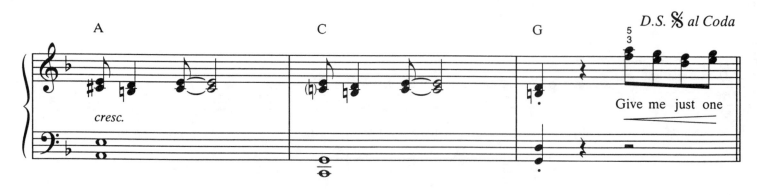

*D.S. 𝄋 al Coda*

Give me just one

*Coda*

# VICTORY CELEBRATION

Music by
JOHN WILLIAMS
*Arranged by DAN COATES*

Victory Celebration - 3 - 1

Victory Celebration - 3 - 3

# WE'RE OFF TO SEE THE WIZARD
## (The Wonderful Wizard of Oz)

Lyric by
E.Y. HARBURG

Music by
HAROLD ARLEN
*Arranged by DAN COATES*

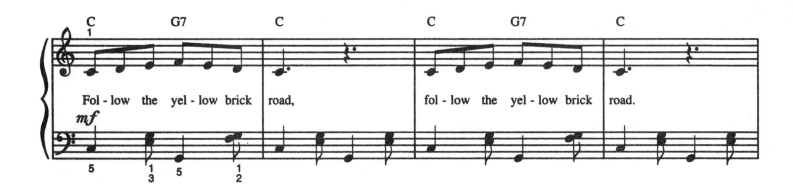

Fol - low the yel - low brick road, fol - low the yel - low brick road.

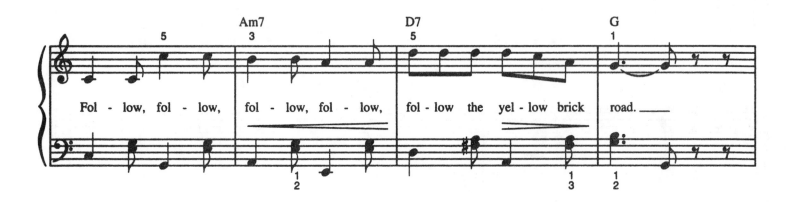

Fol - low, fol - low, fol - low, fol - low, fol - low the yel - low brick road. ____

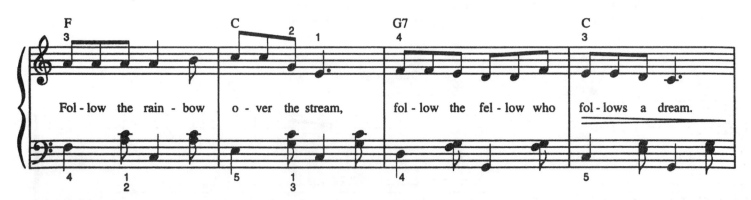

Fol - low the rain - bow o - ver the stream, fol - low the fel - low who fol - lows a dream.

We're Off to See the Wizard - 3 - 1

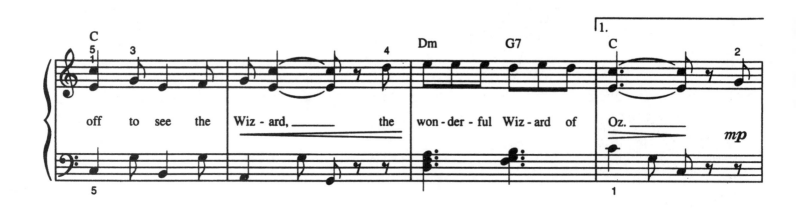

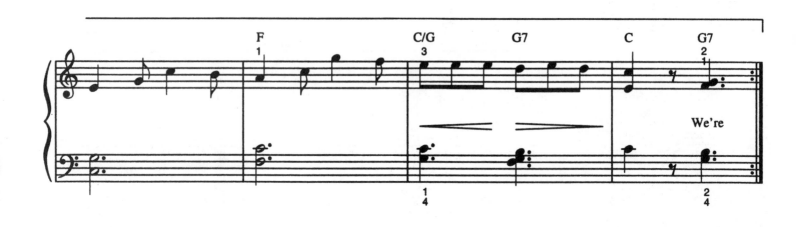

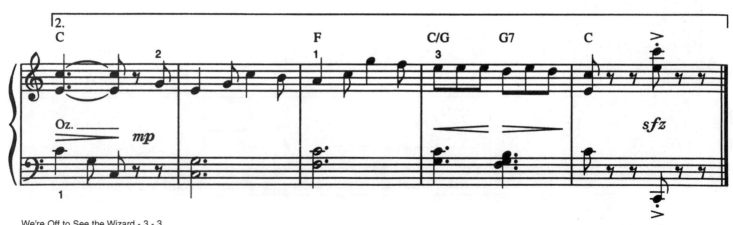

# DAN COATES

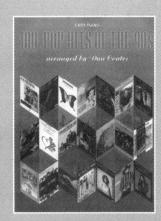

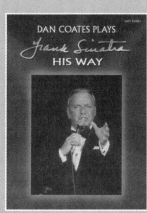
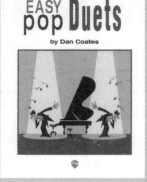
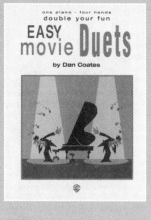

AD0139   Printed in USA

# Intermediate/Advanced Piano Music
## from
# Dan Coates

### Best in Standards (Revised), Book 2
**(PF0542)**

All the Way • Lullaby of Birdland • Secret Love • Sweet Georgia Brown • Three Coins in the Fountain • As Time Goes By • Misty • What's New? • Night and Day • That's All.

### The Best of Broadway
**(PF0871)**

Creative arrangements of Broadway's very best from *Barnum, The Pajama Game, The Will Rogers Follies, City of Angels* and more. Titles include: The Colors of My Life • Corner of the Sky • Favorite Son • If My Friends Could See Me Now • My Unknown Someone • Send in the Clowns • She Loves Me.

### Best of the '70s & '80s
**(PF0768)**

Arthur's Theme (Best That You Can Do) • Brian's Song • Come in from the Rain • How Do You Keep the Music Playing? • Hymne • If • I'll Still Be Loving You • One Moment in Time • The Rose • Saving All My Love for You and more.

### The Best in Christmas Music Complete
**(PF0735A)**

Includes: Christmas Auld Lang Syne • The Christmas Waltz • God Rest Ye Merry Gentlemen • (There's No Place Like) Home for the Holidays • I Heard the Bells on Christmas Day • It Came Upon the Midnight Clear • Let It Snow! Let It Snow! Let It Snow! • Rockin' Around the Christmas Tree • Rudolph the Red-Nosed Reindeer and more.

### The Best in Pops, Book 1
**(PF0187)**

Thirteen top hits including: Up Where We Belong • As Time Goes By • We've Got Tonight • How Do You Keep the Music Playing? • Chariots of Fire and many more.

### The Best in Pops, Book 4
**(PF0608)**

Includes: Anne's Theme • Friends & Lovers (Both to Each Other) • Hymne • I'll Still Be Loving You • Kei's Song • Till I Loved You (Love Theme from *Goya*).

### The Best in Pops, Book 5
**(PF0756)**

Alone in the World • Ashokan Farewell • The Colors of My Life • Get Here • The Gift of Love • (Everything I Do) I Do It for You • I Love to See You Smile • On My Way to You • Summer Me, Winter Me • When You Tell Me That You Love Me.

### The Best in Popular Sheet Music
**(AF9736)**

Contains: Angel Eyes • Because You Loved Me • Desperado • From a Distance • The Greatest Love of All • (Everything I Do) I Do It for You • I Can Love You Like That • I Swear • If You Believe • Stairway to Heaven • Un-Break My Heart • Valentine and 10 more.

### Dan Coates Popular Music Collection for the Advanced Player
**(AF9555)**

An advanced-level book that contains a dozen sophisticated arrangements, including: Angel Eyes • For Love Alone • The Greatest Love of All • I Can Love You Like That • I Swear • New York, New York • Over the Rainbow • The Rose • Tears in Heaven • Theme from *Love Affair* and more.

### Dan Coates Popular Music Collection for the Advanced Player, Volume II
**(AF9754)**

A dozen challenging settings which will provide hours of pleasure for pianists at the advanced level. Includes: Because You Loved Me • Beauty and the Beast • Canon in D • Desperado • Hey, There • If You Believe • Send in the Clowns • Un-Break My Heart • Valentine.

### Fantastic TV & Movie Songs (Revised Edition)
**(PF0925)**

Great television and movie music including: Anywhere the Heart Goes (Meggie's Theme) (from "The Thorn Birds") • Arthur's Theme (Best That You Can Do) (from *Arthur*) • Can You Read My Mind? (Love Theme from *Superman*) • Friends & Lovers (Both to Each Other) (from "Days of Our Lives") • The Rose (from *The Rose*) • Up Where We Belong (from *An Officer and a Gentleman*).

### Great Piano Christmas Hits
**(AF9681)**

An advanced-level book that contains 20 sophisticated Dan Coates arrangements, including: Away in a Manger • Deck the Halls • God Rest Ye Merry Gentlemen • Hark! The Herald Angels Sing • It Came Upon the Midnight Clear • Merry Christmas Darling • Rockin' Around the Christmas Tree • Silent Night • Sleigh Ride.

### Great Popular Music of the '80s
**(PF0621)**

Contains: Always on My Mind • Can't Fight This Feeling • Hymne • I'll Still Be Loving You • Nothing's Gonna Change My Love for You • Once Before I Go • The Search Is Over • We Are the World • The Wind Beneath My Wings and more.

### Great Popular Piano Hits, Volume 2
**(F3050P9X)**

Eight beautiful intermediate piano arrangements of some of our most popular titles like: Corner of the Sky • Didn't We • The Entertainer • The Greatest Love of All • Three Times a Lady • You Light Up My Life.

### I Just Can't Stop Loving You & 16 Romantic Ballads
**(PF0940)**

The ever-popular Dan Coates provides the intermediate to advanced player with creative melodic arrangements of some of today's most enduring love songs. Selections include: As Time Goes By • The Homecoming • Misty • That's What Friends Are For • Up Where We Belong • We've Got Tonight and many more.

### My All-Time Favorite Melodies
**(PF0824)**

All the Way • Alone in the World • Ashokan Farewell • Brian's Song • Color the Children • The Homecoming • How Do You Keep the Music Playing? • If • In Finding You, I Found Love • Misty • Theme from *Nicholas and Alexandra* • The Rose • Time in a Bottle • We've Got Tonight • The Wind Beneath My Wings and more.

### The New Dan Coates Professional Touch Encyclopedia (Revised)
**(PF0562B)**

Includes: Saving All My Love for You • Separate Lives (Love Theme from *White Nights*) • That's What Friends Are For • Send in the Clowns • Open Arms • (Everything I Do) I Do It for You • Up Where We Belong • The Wind Beneath My Wings • Eye of the Tiger • I Swear • The Rose • Stairway to Heaven and much more.

### The Rose & 49 Top Professional Touch Hits
**(PF0826A)**

Anne's Theme • As Time Goes By • Can You Read My Mind? • Evergreen • From a Distance • I Just Can't Stop Loving You • Nothing's Gonna Change My Love for You • One Moment in Time • Send in the Clowns • We Are the World • What's New? and more.

### The Wind Beneath My Wings and 9 Piano Solos
**(PF0698)**

Includes: Can You Read My Mind? (Love Theme from *Superman*) • How Do You Keep the Music Playing? • Hymne • Kei's Song • Miss Celie's Blues (Sister) • Missing (Theme from *Missing*) • Noelle's Theme (The Other Side of Midnight) • Once Before I Go • One Moment in Time and title song.